MIRA

Glimpses of Life & Whispers from the Heart

A Collection of Mira(cle)Doodles - Volume 1

Dedicated to your inner child.
May she always find a joyful way
to follow your heart!

Doodles #1-31 are drawn based on INKTOBER 2018 prompts
Doodles #32-62 are drawn based on INKTOBER 2019 prompts

Disclaimer: The information shared in this book is for educational and informational purposes only and is not intended to be viewed as medical or mental health advice. It is not designed to be a substitute for professional advice from your physician, therapist, attorney, accountant or any other health care practitioner or licensed professional. The Publisher and the Author do not make any guarantees as to the effectiveness of any of the techniques, suggestions, tips, ideas or strategies shared in this book as each situation differs. The Publisher and Author shall neither have liability nor responsibility with respect to any direct or indirect loss or damage caused or alleged by the information shared in this book related to your health, life or business or any other aspect of your situation. It's your responsibility to do your own due diligence and use your own judgment when applying any techniques or situations mentioned in or through this book. Any citations or sources of information from other organizations or websites are not endorsements of the information or content the website or organization provides or recommendations it may make. Please be aware that that any websites or references that were available during publication may not be available in the future.

Sometimes life feels like a never-ending struggle to choose between Good and Bad. You feel pulled to do the right thing, but screw up again and again, because life's messy.

These doodles were drawn from the need to shift from repeating the same old unconscious patterns and to access a new level of happiness. They were drawn daily in October 2018 and 2019, inspired by the one-word prompts of Jake Parker's INKTOBER challenge. The doodles are presented in the same order as the prompts were given, and present my musings on the journey from day 1 to day 62, with four short stories in between.

All of the doodles made my day one at a time as they popped out of my pen and made me smile. I even enjoyed the ones that felt like a gentle slap on the face, asking me to wake up and remember to choose Love over fear. With this awareness, choosing Love becomes the obvious choice.

We all have the power to choose to follow our heart. Let's just remember to pause, look around and notice that Love is ever-present.
But if only it was that easy to hear its whispers…

The one thing that sharing my doodles has shown me is that no one is ever alone in this journey—life's messy for all of us. My hope is that this doodle collection will inspire you on your journey toward more happiness!

How about Mira?
Will she choose fear or will she keep
following her heart?

Let's find out!

Meet the Characters

MIRA is an ever-curious, joyful inner child who loves to follow her heart and doesn't stop, even when the ego butts in.

MIRA'S HEART represents inner wisdom. She symbolizes the Love that we are. A Love that is all-encompassing, all-accepting. She knows our birthright is Love, Joy and Ease. The heart never leaves Mira even if she loses sight of it. Love will stick around like the Sun: Clouds may hide the sun, but it still shines.

A LIZARD symbolizes the ego—representing moments when we try to play it safe and make decisions from our primary brain (also called the lizard brain).

It's helpful to remember that the ego always speaks first, and loudest, with its attempts to lead us away from Love.

The ego offers replacements for Love that always leave us wanting for more. Nothing is ever enough for the ego.

Other Symbols Used in This Book

 STARS symbolize miracles, which are shifts in perception according to *A Course in Miracles.* This shift happens when we question the world that the ego shows us and start to wonder if there is another way of looking at the situation we are in. This in itself is a miracle, seeing reality as it is—as Love.

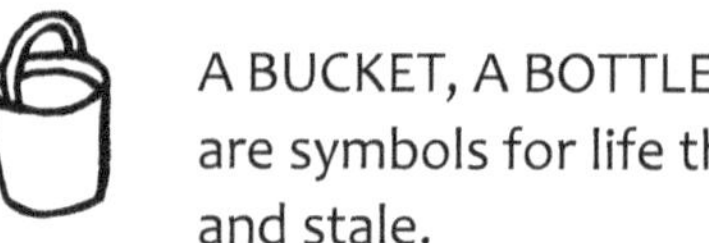 A BUCKET, A BOTTLE & A SNOW GLOBE are symbols for life that feels constricted and stale.

A WHALE represents thoughts that come with emotional baggage and take up space in our lives—consciously or unconsciously.

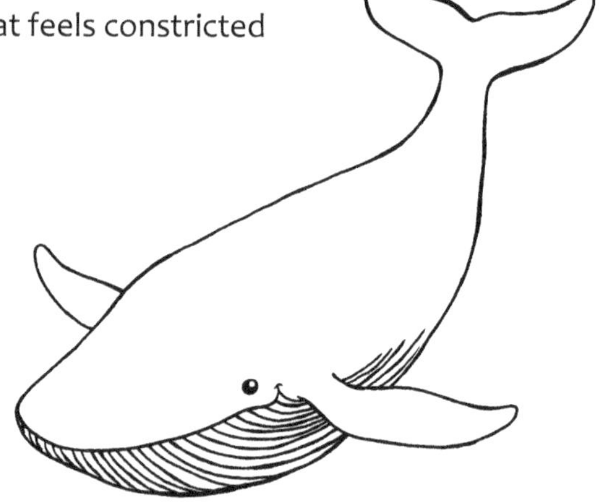

 A PRESENT represents our gifts, strengths, talents and passions.

 A THOUGHT BUBBLE symbolizes thoughts and dreams. When they are drawn as balloons on a string, the thoughts are being brought to our awareness.

A HORSE represents the mind. This is a clumsy symbol, but it works for these doodles. Tame your mind and ride with it to your freedom.

A TREADMILL & A HAMSTER WHEEL represent our modern busy life where hustling is praised, and an overload of stress makes us forget to listen to our heart.

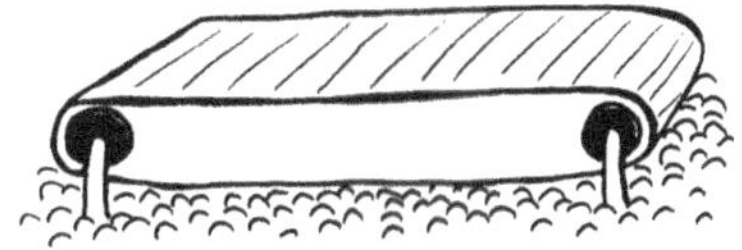

ALL THE SYMBOLS are drawn to help us move forward, towards more light & Love.

Under the cloak is the ego. But is it yours or someone else's?
If you happen to take a bite of a poison apple, you don't need a true
love's kiss to wake from slumber—a self-love's kiss will do!

Even in the tranquil moments of life, it can feel like there's something lurking in the shadows.

Shine your light into all the different parts of yourself— No more secrets!

When you shine the light, there will no longer be parts of you that turn into scary monsters.

How can you turn your ego's fire into something sweet today?

Let what you love light up your path and release you from the spell.

From the ego's point of view,
being a chicken keeps you safe.

But is that what you really came here for?!
Let's not chicken out on the beauty of transformation!

Does your ego sometimes make you feel
like you're wasting your talents?

When Love leads,
the ego can't keep up.
Bliss!

"Shoot for the moon.
Even if you miss, you'll
land among the stars."
- Norman Vincent Peale

My...
Precious!

What will you do with this
precious life that is yours?
Will you listen to your ego or
follow your soul?

When this little girl was born, ego looked
at Love and started a race.
Well, of course the ego won—it was
the only one competing and it's always
louder and more obvious.

All the while Love just stood there,
looking lovingly at Mira.

And in the end,
that's way more
powerful.

The ego may offer her a nice little bucket of life,
but into the flow she jumps instead, following her heart.
What kind of jump can you take today to make your life flow more freely?

Sometimes it feels like one part of me
has turned against me.
How cruel is that?!

A SHORT STORY

What You Focus on Grows

- The Story of a Whale Under My Rug -

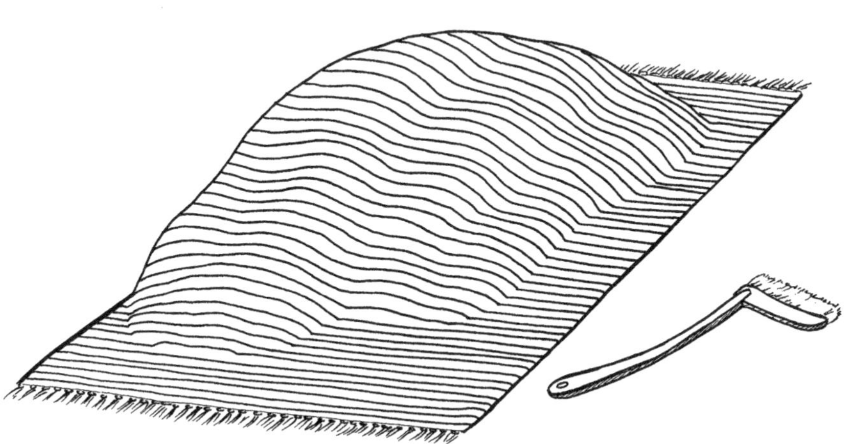

There's a saying, "What you focus on, grows."
But what if there's a whale under my rug?

It's hard not to focus on it...

And it grows and grows.
What on earth is it doing there anyway...?
Well, that's not my business... I'll take it back to
where it belongs and try to focus on other things.

I wonder though,
how did it end up under my rug?
How is it even possible?
Naah, I decided to stop worrying and
let go of my need to analyze this.

Next, I found a light house on the beach.
My heart asked me to take a closer look.
"A human mind is like a light house," she said.

"Your mind has a dark cellar filled
with murky secrets
you can dwell upon for years,
but it also has potential to light up
the sky at night."

"Hold on to the Source
of your light,
and choose what you
want to shine it upon!"

When I finally reached the top to light up the sky...

Oops!
The whale was back again.

But now, holding my light,
I said:
"I'm ready!
I'm present.
I am listening.
Be my teacher.

Show me
the reason why
you're here."

It's in there?

Okay,
I'll be brave...

In the depths of the whale,
I saw the bigger picture and lit it up with my love.
I realized... it no longer had power over me.

I was freed.
What I previously saw as a problem,
something I wanted to hide...
Now just made me smile.
I carry it with me proudly.
And it's kinda cute!

I trust my heart.
I will follow her.
Nooo! Don't do it! You'll fall!
It's okay!

Even with being so well-guarded by the ego,
wouldn't you rather jump and trust your heart?

Oh, but I don't need your clock & timers, or your bells & whistles! I've got my body, the sun, the moon and the stars.

Listening to my body lets me know when it's time
to eat, sleep, create, exercise, stretch...

With the Moon as my guide, I can learn when it's wise to
slow down, plant seeds, shine and let go.

The stars, just like miracles, help me find my way,
and the Sun keeps reminding me how it's possible to
shine my light on everything and for everyone.

Yep, in the end even the most stubborn ego will relax when Love leads.

Keep following your heart!

Let's outsmart the ego and see through its "presents".

What have you done?
I enjoyed a good round of commenting on social media for you.

Do you ever feel battered after
spending time on social media?
Sadly, hate and negativity sells.

What if we
spread Love
instead?

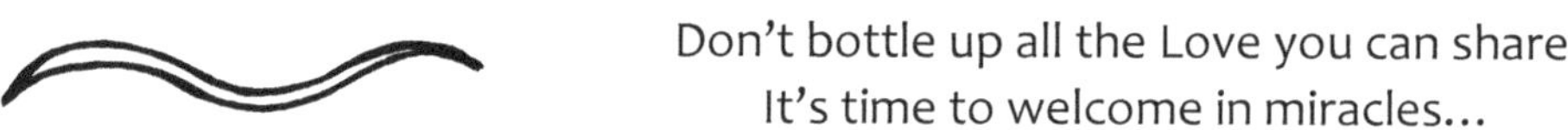

Don't bottle up all the Love you can share.
It's time to welcome in miracles…

…And let them show you where to go!

It's the ego that can break, not Love.

Have you read the small print and considered the cost for signing a contract with the ego?

Let your heart lead, and you'll feel the difference!

When price tags stop you from going for your dreams,
remember that the best things in life
are not expensive at all!
Stop standing on your own way.
Allow your next miracle to appear!

When life gets muddy,
make mud cakes!
When the ego keeps

dumping in more mud,
hear your heart's whisper:

Play with me!

Umm... O-k-a-y...
See, it starts to make sense.

What comes to mind with this prompt?
Chopping wood!
What if Mira was chopping her thoughts
into pieces with her ego?

No matter how small you make
your thoughts in an attempt to find
underlying meanings,
you waste your time.

All you really need is to step back and look for Love.
It's right there waiting for you.

If you are struggling
with your ego,
be patient.

Don't be threatened
by its prickliness.

You know what? I could love you to pieces...

Be willing to stretch for
what you want.
You've got all you need.

Stretch to remember
your dream.

Stretch to say "No" if it's not
what you really want and need.

Stretch to be you.
Just for you.

Stretch towards Love.
Eventually, it gets easier.

Rrrumbble...
I'm pretty sure I've heard that before...

Like thunderstorms,
the drama in your life is
meant to pass.

Learn to recognize the sound of thunder,
but pay more attention to
the whispers of your heart.

Unwrap your gifts and give it a go!

You thought it was your heart calling, but you better
double check it this time.

Suddenly a jolt of
surprise pushed
her forward.

... And that's how she learned to fly.

The best way to really dream…
… is to let your dream become part of you.

And how is this different from the doodle (#24)
where the ego disected Mira's thought into
smaller parts to analyze it?

The ego looked at it from the outside.

Letting the dreams you dream with Love
become one with you is much more
efficient and fun!

But you DO have your heart on speed dial. You truly do.
Even if your ego is louder, your heart's closer.

When Love takes the mind for a ride,
they sure have fun!

See, this is how to do it.
I bet she can't resist this thought!

Do you fight, flight or freeze when
your ego gets offended?
When the ego reacts, it's hard to
remember to ask what Love would do….

If you feel stuck, it may be comforting to know that one third of a skyscraper is below the ground.

The bigger the dream, the
deeper it's okay to dig
for sturdy foundations.
Imagine, how strong it will be!
Ask yourself: am I stuck, or am I building my dream?

Keep choosing your own kind of journey!

The way you want to travel through this journey called life is your own unique decision. Keep going for it—Invite joy to pull you forward!

Ta-dah!

A Castle in the Clouds

The ego knows
how to keep me busy dreaming,
and building castles in the clouds.

But do I really need a castle?

It's almost as if I was enchanted
by the ego,

until…

Oops...

Until the truth was revealed.
Ego's illusions are fragile, and when
they are exposed, it hurts.
But then I remember it's the ego
who suffers, not me.

Now the question is, will I allow the ego to find
another way to distract me from the truth?

Or would I rather build my life with Love?

The moment when the ego realized
it's too frail without Love.

I'd rather play with Love…

Oops, I can spot a pattern there...
It's in the past. Look at the bigger picture and follow me!
Conscious Incompetence
Conscious Competence
Unconscious Incompetence (START)
Unconscious Competence (GOAL)
Consciousness
Competence

How hard it can be to learn new skills when you
try and try and try, but keep slipping back to
your old habits and ignorance.

Learning gets easier when you see
the big picture. You just first need
to dance a bit of cha cha cha before
you get there!

This model is called The Learning Stages Model and was developed by Noel Burch
from Gordon Training International. I found this version called the Conscious
Competence Matrix from the Mind Tools website.

At first it felt impossible to hear whispers from the heart
because the wall was so thick.
Slowly the wall became transparent and I learned
to trust that there's more to life than it seemed.

There's a whole Universe full of possibilities!

What are you going
to dress up as
for Halloween?
A dragon,
of course!

Oh boy, how the ego would love to be
a fierce, brave, strong dragon—ah,
all that grandiose dragon stuff.
But all it got was a costume...

Rise Like a Phoenix

I tend to go all in and…

... burn out.

Now what?

Who gets to help me rise from the ashes this time?

And like a phoenix I rise.

Here we go again!

- THE END -
or THE BEGINNING (again)

An overgrown ego flattens the world,
whereas Love lifts it up and keeps expanding.

You could become Legendary!
But...
Don't mind him. Let's just go do our thing.

What if the cure for
the racing mind is acceptance?
I've come to accept that some nights
I soar the skies with my mind.
The next day I accept that I can
be a bit more tired.
And to my surprise, I typically have the time
of my life after a night like that.

Accepting yourself the way you are recharges
your batteries, too (just like sleep)!

What does that even mean "ornament"?
I'll just skip this prompt...

Maybe no one notices,
the ego wishes.

Curiously enough,
most of the times,
no one does.

When you think there's something wrong with you
and that you don't fit in...

Look for the world made with Love!

The ego may think it's getting rid of a nuisance…
But how can you get rid of something that's
all-encompassing?

Love already is everywhere.

I think I'm stuck!
I'll never get there!
Ah, don't you worry! I'll speed it up a notch and you'll be okay! (As if...)
CLICK

What if you stopped and asked yourself,
did you even want a carrot in the first place?

She can't see that her heart
already has it figured out…

The ego makes her see
a long and dangerous
journey instead.

When You Find Yourself
in a Nightmare…

There once was a little girl who
had horrible nightmares.

She kept waking up night after night in a cold sweat.
She was too horrified to open her eyes.
What if the ghosts were still there?

She wasn't brave enough to cry for help.
She just waited for the night to end.

Until…

Until the day came when she decided that she had had enough. No more nightmares for her.

Her determination shined so brightly that when she laid her head on the pillow that night, and the usual nightmare started to take shape in her dreams, she realized that something had changed. She walked those dark and deserted corridors of her nightmare. She saw the ghosts approach, and instead of horror weakening her knees, she felt a tingling in her stomach.

It expanded and grew until it touched her heart and she laughed a little. The ghosts looked puzzled and retreated at the sound. It looked so funny that she laughed a bit more, and then more, until she was on the floor rolling with laughter in her dream. And poof! The nightmare disappeared. The ghosts never came back.

If life's a dream, does it mean that I can start laughing and wake up at any given moment? Even right now?

- THE END -

The question is ancient…

Which to follow…
…fear or Love?

Not before I stepped off of the hamster wheel of my life did
I notice how dizzy it actually had made me feel... Woah!

The moment she got curious about
what Love has to offer...

It's good to sometimes imagine yourself sitting on a bench,
eating popcorn and watching yourself from afar as if in a movie,
simply observing your behavior.

What happens in the next scene?
Ask your heart.

"If you don't have a shadow, you
are standing in darkness."
- Deepak Chopra

If the ego hadn't jumped to quick conclusions, it would have understood that Mira may have made a little mistake in pronunciation.

Let's enjoy the ride—Now!

Stop fighting.
Try Loving!

Here's to trying again and trusting that
the Universe has your back!

You were right
—it IS easy when
the timing is right!

Everything becomes more effortless when
you stop rushing and pushing.

Fruits always
taste better
when they are
ripe.

DOODLING MIRACLES
- INSPIRING JOY & REFLECTION -

Mira(cle)Doodles are illustrations from a spiritual path,
born from a need to question the ego's ways and
to follow the heart no matter what comes your way.
Inspired by inner musings about life, they simplify and
explain life's struggles and spiritual challenges with a loving
twist. They show how it's possible to choose Love and
be at peace in any moment.

The doodles help you connect with your own inner wisdom
and inspire you to expand into a deeper understanding of
life and Love.

WWW.DOODLINGMIRACLES.COM

ABOUT THE AUTHOR & ILLUSTRATOR

Elina Puohiniemi, aka elinap, is an artist, life coach and
the creator of the Mira(cle)Doodles series.

She has been illustrating her spiritual path with doodles
since 2010. For the past nine years, she has explored
life with her doodle character, Mira, in her
(almost) daily doodling.

She lives in Finland with her husband, their
two teenage sons and a poodle.

Ingram Content Group UK Ltd.
Milton Keynes UK
UKHW050236210323
418837UK00003B/10